The American Bison

by Steve Potts

Reading Consultant:
Norm Bishop
Resources Interpreter
Yellowstone National Park

CAPSTONE BOOKS
an imprint of Capstone Press
Mankato, Minnesota

Capstone Books are published by Capstone Press
151 Good Counsel Drive, P.O. Box 669, Mankato, Minnesota 56002
http://www.capstone-press.com

Printed in the United States of America.

Library of Congress Cataloging-in-Publication Data
Potts, Steve, 1956-
The American bison/by Steve Potts.
p. cm.--(Wildlife of North America)
Includes bibliographical references (p. 46) and index.
Summary: Details the characteristics, habitat, and life cycle of the American bison.
ISBN 1-56065-468-6
1. The American bison--Juvenile literature. [1. Bison.] I. Title. II. Series.
QL737.U53P68 1997
595.64'3'O97--dc21

96-48686
CIP
AC

Photo credits
Visuals Unlimited/W. Weber, cover
William Muñoz, 6, 10, 12, 17, 20, 24-28, 36
Lynn M. Stone, 8, 14, 18, 22, 30-34, 38-44

Table of Contents

Pronunciation guides follow difficult words, both in the text and in the Words to Know section in the back of the book.

Fast Facts about the American Bison

Scientific Name: Bison bison bison

Length: Bison measure about 11 and one-half feet (three and one-half meters) in length.

Height: Bison stand about six feet (two meters) in height, measuring from the ground to the hump.

Weight: Bison weigh about 2,000 pounds (907 kilograms).

Habitat: Bison prefer grasslands and open prairies. Today most bison live on ranches, farms, or wildlife refuges.

Food: Bison are herbivores (HUR-buh-vorz). Herbivores are animals that eat plants. Bison eat mostly prairie grasses and plants.

Habits: Bison are social animals. They travel in herds and have a keen sense of smell.

Reproduction: Female bison are called cows. Cows give birth in May. The calves live with the cow for up to three years. Calves are newborn bison.

Range: Bison once roamed North America. Now, herds are only found in small areas, such as parks and game preserves.

Life Span: Bison usually live to be between 13 and 15 years old. But they may live as long as 25 or 30 years.

State Animal: Bison is the state animal for Oklahoma and Kansas.

State Mammal: Bison is the state mammal for Wyoming.

Chapter 1

The American Bison

The American bison is one of the world's largest mammals. Mammals are warm-blooded animals with backbones. Mammals also nurse their young.

In 1700, 30 million to 60 million bison roamed the plains of North America. Their range stretched from the west coast to as far east as Virginia and Pennsylvania. A range is an area where animals hunt. By 1832, no bison lived east of the Mississippi River. By 1900, only about 250 wild bison roamed the face of North America.

At one time, 30 million bison roamed the plains.

A male bison weighs about 1,800 pounds (810 kilograms).

The once large herds of bison disappeared when settlers arrived in North America. Settlers owned horses and guns. They could kill more bison than North American Indians, who used bows and arrows.

North American Indians relied on bison to survive. They never wasted their kill. They ate the meat, used the skins for clothing and tepees, and made tools from the bones. Unlike North American Indians, settlers often killed bison for their tongues and hides. They left the rest of the bison's body to fade into bones.

Eventually, people became concerned about the disappearing bison. Bison were saved from extinction. Extinction means that a type of plant or animal is in danger of dying out. A few dozen survived in Yellowstone National Park. Today, about 100,000 bison live in wildlife refuges or on private ranches in North America.

Bison Characteristics

Male bison are called bulls. On average, they weigh about 1,800 pounds (810 kilograms). They stand about six feet (180 centimeters) tall, measuring from the ground to the hump.

Scat, pictured below, is used to find out where an animal lives and what it eats.

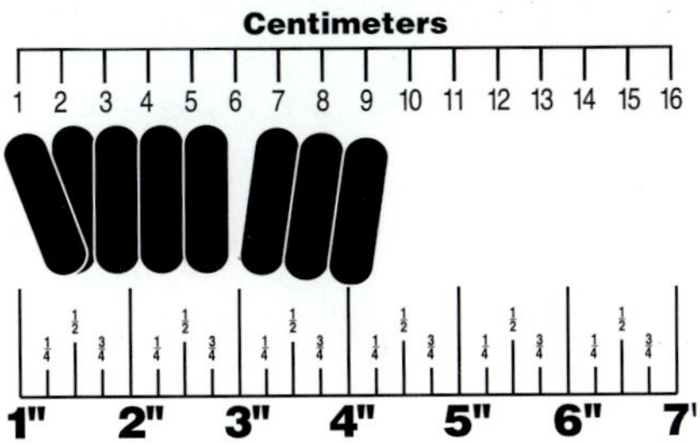

Female bison are called cows. They are smaller than bulls. They weigh about 800 to 1,000 pounds (360 to 450 kilograms). They stand about five feet (150 centimeters) tall from the ground to the hump.

Newborn bison are called calves. They weigh between 30 and 40 pounds (13-1/2 and 18 kilograms) at birth. Bison usually live to be between 13 and 15 years. But they may live up to 25 or 30 years.

Bison have beards of rough, stringy fur that hang down below their mouths. They have horns that curve upward and toward their heads.

Bison's skulls have two layers of heavy bone. These layers cushion their brains against any shock. The bones also protect the bison from a hunter's bullets.

Bison have cloven hooves. Cloven hooves are round with a split in the center. Bison's eyes are a reddish color. Their tails have a short tuft of hair.

The muscles in a bison's neck and hump help support its huge head. In the winter, these muscles help it push away snow. Then it can eat grass buried underneath the snow.

Bison have beards that hang below their mouths.

Chapter 2

The Seasons

Bison go through several physical changes throughout the year. Their activities also change with the seasons.

Spring

In early spring, bison shed their heavy winter coats. This shedding is called molting (MOHLT-ing).

To remove the hair, bison rub their bodies against any objects they can find. They rub against big rocks, fence posts, and trees. Bison rub so hard they strip off tree bark up to six feet (180 centimeters) from the ground. A herd

In spring, bison shed their winter coats.

Bison roll in dust and mud to smother biting insects.

of bison once pushed down a wooden cabin while rubbing off their fur.

A bison's fur comes off in patches. Some of the heavier winter coat remains on a bison's legs and back. The heavier hair looks like short pants. The new hair that grows in is lighter brown, shorter, and stiffer than the winter coat.

The short, stiff hair sticks out from the bison's skin. Then air can move more freely between the hair and skin. This helps bison stay cool on the hot summer plains.

Summer

Insects and flies bother bison during summer months. To get rid of them, bison wallow. This means they roll around in the dust or mud. The dust and mud help smother biting flies and insects.

Bison wallow in the same area for many years. Their wallowing wears the ground. The worn ground looks like a giant bowl. It is also called a wallow. Some wallows have existed more than 100 years. Between rolling, rubbing, and scratching, the bison relieve the itching caused by insects.

Fall

During late summer and fall, bison prepare for winter. Their light summer coat gradually changes. It turns into a thick, dark brown covering that will protect them against the snow.

A bison's winter coat has two layers. On top is a layer of thick hairs. Underneath is a layer of woolly fur that keeps in warmth and keeps out the damp cold. Together, these two layers help the bison survive cold, snowy prairie winters.

Surviving Winter

In the 1700s, bison traveled in herds of thousands across the plains. Winter survival required special preparation in these times. In the late fall and winter, bison separated into smaller groups. The adult bulls formed groups of 10 to 25 animals. Cows and calves came together in groups of 20 to 60. The small groups made it easier to find food. They also provided protection from the cold wind.

During fall and winter, these groups looked for food. They gathered and divided several times during the winter.

Today bison already travel in smaller groups within protected wild areas. But finding food in winter still is challenging.

Bison need to move snow to survive. They use their noses, hooves, and heads to push snow off the grass they eat. Bison can live in snow up to four feet (120 centimeters) deep.

During winter, bison have a harder time finding food.

Chapter 3

Bison Habits

Bison's survival depends upon their instincts. Instincts are behaviors that are natural rather than learned. Some of the bison's instincts have changed over time. Others remain the same.

Migration

When bison roamed the prairies in great numbers, they developed a pattern of migration (MYE-gray-shun). Migration means that animals move to a new living area for feeding or breeding.

Bison migrated during the year to find enough food. After migrating, bison would find

Bison once traveled across the plains to new living areas to find food.

and claim a range. A range is a wide area of open ground. They searched the range for food.

Often, bison migrated to hills and mountains in the spring and summer. There, they found plenty of water and grass. The temperatures were much cooler.

In the fall and winter, they walked to the lower prairies to find food. The prairies had less snow over the grasses and plants that bison ate. Bison generally traveled one to two miles (one and one-half to three kilometers) during the winter in their search for food and water.

Today bison living in a wildlife refuge such as Yellowstone Park do not migrate. During winter, bison travel in groups to the lower parts of the park.

There, shade from trees keeps the snow from melting and freezing, so the snow stays soft. Bison need to find the softer snow, so they can push it away. Then, they can eat the grasses.

Bison survive mostly on native grasses. They are ruminants. This means they chew

Bison survive mostly on native grasses.

their cud. Cud is regurgitated (ree-GUR-juh-tate-ed) food. They swallow their food and digest part of it in one of their four stomachs. Then they bring the cud back up to their mouths to chew again. They repeat this process until their food is completely digested.

Mating Time

In July, bison are ready to rut. Rut means breed. When breeding season starts, the stronger bison show dominance over other bison. Dominance means to control or rule. Only a few of the strongest bulls mate. Since only a few cows are ready to breed, bulls must fight for a cow.

Sometimes younger bulls will challenge older, stronger bulls. The stronger bulls will snort, sneeze, grunt, or bellow. These noises are sometimes enough to frighten challengers away. If not, the stronger bulls will stare at the other bulls or swing their horns toward them.

If the challengers still refuse to move away, stronger bulls will bellow, snort, and paw at the ground. They may also charge the other bulls

Bison calves stay close to their mothers after they are born.

Bison stampede when they are threatened.

and ram their heads against them. The fighting continues until one of the bulls gives up.

Once a bull has established his dominance, he seeks cows for breeding. During mating in July, a bull tends one cow at a time. He tries to keep her from other bulls in the herd. The bull tends cows as little as a few minutes or for as long as a few days.

Cows give birth after nine and one-half months. Most cows have their first calf when they are three years old. Cows have calves every year if food is plentiful. If there is little food, cows give birth every other year.

Bison calves are usually born in April or May. They stay close to their mothers for a month after they are born. When they are one month old, calves leave their mothers for most of the day. They continue to nurse for eight months to a year. By their first winter, the mother and calf spend little time together.

Temperament

Bison may seem like gentle, quiet animals. But they can become angry. When humans or other animals come near bison calves, older bison will chase them away. Bison can jump over barriers and use their bodies like bulldozers. They can run up to speeds of 35 miles (56 kilometers) per hour.

Centuries ago, large herds of bison would sometimes stampede across the plains. A stampede would happen when a herd of bison ran from what they thought was danger. Stampedes often occurred when bison heard thunder or saw lightning.

North American Indians depended on bison for food.

Bison would also stampede when they saw or smelled something that threatened them. Once they began running, bison would not stop until they reached a safe place. Usually they looked for trees or a place on a small hill. There they felt protected.

Today bison do not stampede across the prairie. They do, however, become easily frightened by strange sights, sounds, and smells. Visitors to Yellowstone Park need to be aware that bison can be easily alarmed and start running. Visitors may be in danger of being trampled if they come too close to them.

Sense of Smell

Bison have a very good sense of smell. Bison's eyesight and hearing are not as good. It is their ability to smell that warns them of danger.

In the 1600s and 1700s, North American Indians hunted bison for food. The Indians always approached bison from downwind. They learned to cover themselves with coyote or wolf skins to fool the bison. The smell of the animal skins covered up the human scent.

Indian hunters could sneak within a few feet or meters of the bison. Later, North American Indians had horses and guns. This made hunting easier.

Chapter 4

A Bison Myth

After the ice age, the North American Indians relied on bison to survive. The ice age was a period of time in history when ice covered the earth. Most animals did not survive the ice age. Bison were one of the few large animals that survived the ice age. Indians hunted them mostly for meat.

Indians also depended on the bison for clothing and supplies. Bison bones were used to make tools. Bison skin was made into tepees and clothing. Indians used bison fur to make robes, so they would be warm in the winter.

Bison were one of the few large animals that survived the ice age.

Bison have always had an important role in the life of North America Indians.

The Sacred White Buffalo

The Lakota Sioux Indians (la-KO-ta SUE) have a myth about a white bison. A myth is a story that gives reasons for something that happens in nature. The white bison myth says that many Lakota Sioux came together to camp. The sun was hot, and the campers had no food. They were starving. So two young men went out on a hunt. The two men met a beautiful woman dressed in white. She seemed to float as she walked.

One of the men tried to touch her. He turned into a pile of bones. She told the other man to let his people know that she was coming.

She came and gave the people a sacred pipe. She taught them how to use it in a prayer. She told the Sioux about the value of the bison. She also said that women and children of the tribe were from Mother Earth. She said they were as great as the warriors.

Before she left, she told the people she would return. She then walked away and turned into a white bison calf. The Lakota Sioux honored their pipe by using it, and bison were plentiful.

In August 1994, a white bison calf was born in Janesville, Wisconsin. Many believe the calf symbolizes the coming together of humanity.

Chapter 5

Bison's Future

The first white settlers were amazed at the number of bison. Huge herds roamed the plains. Some early explorers counted thousands of bison in a single herd. Thirty million to 60 million bison once lived in North America.

As settlers moved West, they killed off many bison. By 1800, there were few bison left east of the Mississippi River. Soon, they began to disappear in the West as well. Thousands of bison were killed to feed railroad workers. Railroad workers spent days on the western plains. They helped lay down the first train tracks across the United States.

By 1800, the large herds of bison began to disappear.

Some people worried that bison would become extinct.

Bison often knocked down fences and tore up crops, so farmers killed them. People in Eastern cities liked bison robes, and combs and buttons made of bison bones. By 1900, almost no bison were left in North America.

The Endangered Bison

In the early 1900s, people began to worry that the bison would become extinct. Two of these people were Frederick Dupree (DOO-pree) and

Charles B. Jones. Dupree was a rancher from Kansas, and Jones was a rancher from South Dakota. They worried that the bison would completely die out.

Dupree and Jones captured small groups of bison. They began to sell their bison to zoos, parks, and other ranchers who wanted to raise bison. They helped to create the American Bison Society. This group was dedicated to saving the bison. It wanted to protect 10 national bison herds.

This group's task became much easier when they received support from President Theodore Roosevelt. Roosevelt loved to hunt. He owned a ranch in North Dakota.

Roosevelt thought saving the bison was important. He helped set up herds at the National Zoo in Washington, D.C. He also helped save bison in Yellowstone National Park.

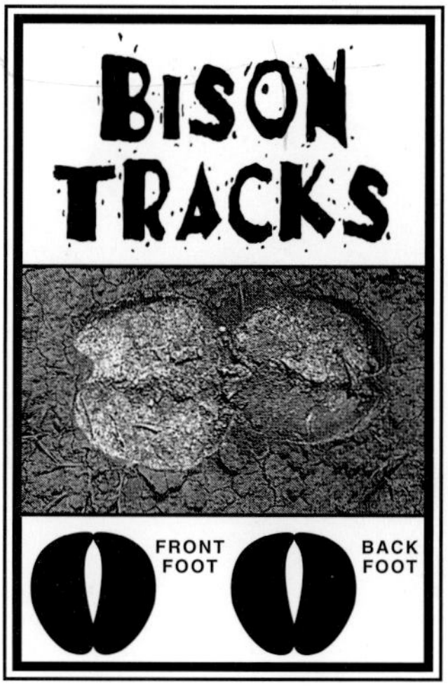

Hump
Curved Horns
Thick Skull
Stringy Beard

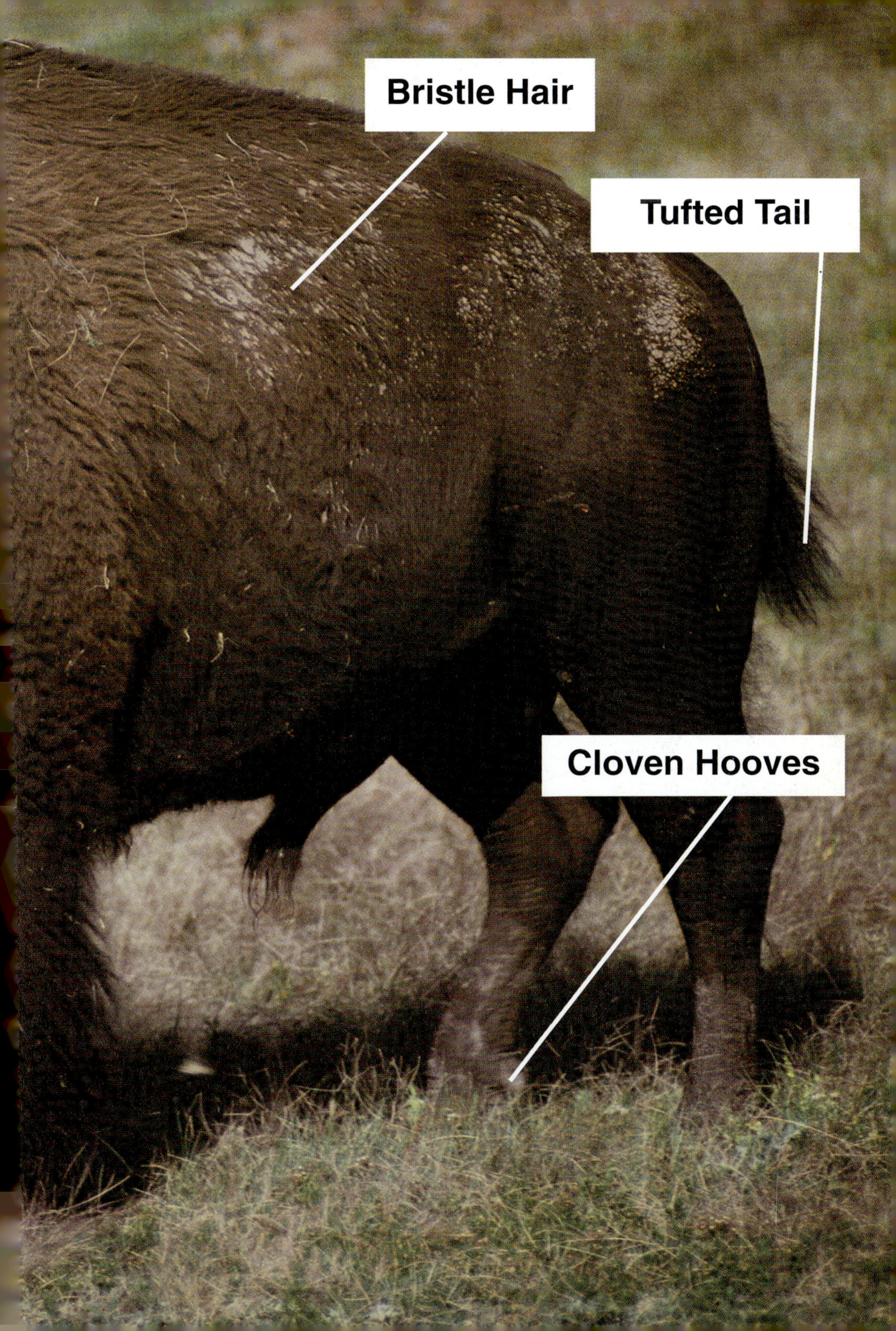
Bristle Hair
Tufted Tail
Cloven Hooves

Where the Bison Live

Bison in Yellowstone National Park

Today large bison herds live in several national parks and wildlife refuges. A wildlife refuge is a park or a forest where animals are not hunted.

Tourists can see bison roaming freely in Yellowstone National Park in Wyoming and Montana. They can see them at Theodore Roosevelt National Park in North Dakota and at Custer State Park in South Dakota. Bison can also be seen at Wood Buffalo National Park in Western Canada.

Several North American Indian groups have also begun to raise bison. Bison meat is low in fat. The groups hope to sell the meat to restaurants. They hope to help save the animals that were so important to their way of life.

Hope for Bison

In recent years, some people have hoped that the bison will again take over the Great Plains. Bison can adapt to the cold winters and hot summers in the West. Bison can also survive on prairie grasses that cattle do not like to eat. Maybe one day there will again be huge herds of bison on the western prairies.

Words to Know

bull (BUL)—an adult male bison
calf (KAF)—a young bison
cow (KOU)—an adult female bison
dominate (DOM-uh-nate)—to control or rule
extinct (ek-STINGKT)—a type of plant or animal that has died out
herbivore (HUR-buh-vor)—an animal that eats plants
instinct (IN-stingkt)—behavior that is natural rather than learned
Lakota Sioux (lah-KO-ta SUE)—Plains Indians that lived in the present-day states of North Dakota, South Dakota, Montana, and Minnesota
migrate (MYE-grate)—to move to a new living area for feeding or breeding
rutting (RUHT-ing)—a mating period
scat (SKAT)—animal droppings

stampede (stam-PEED)—when a herd of animals runs from what they think is danger

tepee (TEE-pee)—a tent shaped like a cone made from animal skins

wallow (WAHL-oh)—to roll around in dust and mud; worn ground that looks like a giant bowl

wildlife refuge (WILDE-life REF-yooj)—a park where animals cannot be hunted

To Learn More

Stone, Lynn M. *Bison Farms*. Funky Farms. Vero Beach, Fla.: Rourke, 1999.

Taylor, J. David. *The Bison and the Great Plains*. Animals and Their Ecosystems. New York: Crabtree Publishing, 1994.

Wilkinson, Todd. *Bison: Bison Magic for Kids*. Animal Magic for Kids. Milwaukee: Gareth Stevens, 1995.

Wrobel, Scott. *Buffalo*. Northern Trek. Mankato, Minn.: Smart Apple Media, 1999.

Some people hope that the bison will one day return to the plains of North America.

Useful Addresses

American Bison Association
P.O. Box 965
Cody, WY 57730

Canadian Buffalo Association
P. O. Box 129
Earlton, ON P0J 1E0
Canada

Intertribal Bison Cooperative
2460 Deadwood Ave
P.O. Box 8105
Rapid City, SD 57709-8105

National Bison Association
P.O. Box 706
Custer, SD 57730

Internet Sites

American Bison
http://drew.buffalo.k12.ny.us/drew/tours/zoo/Bison/bison.html

Bison bison
http://www.oit.itd.umich.edu/projects/adw2k/accounts/bison/b._bison.html$narrative

National Bison Association
http://www.nbabison.org

Native Lore: The Buffalo Rock
http://www.ilhawaii.net/~stony/lore49.html

Index